Creative Scary Halloween

Coloring Book

By

S.B. Nozaz

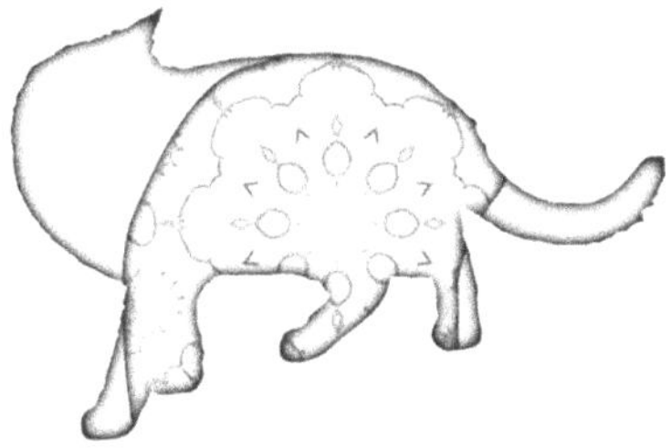

Introduction

Halloween is a great fun time for both children and adults. This fun time can stimulate their imagination about many kinds of Halloween symbols such as goblins, zombies, Dracula, ghosts, , witches, bats, black cats, pumpkins and their special characters. S.B. Nozaz has created this book for everyone who love and would like to enjoy Halloween more and more. Let's try it.

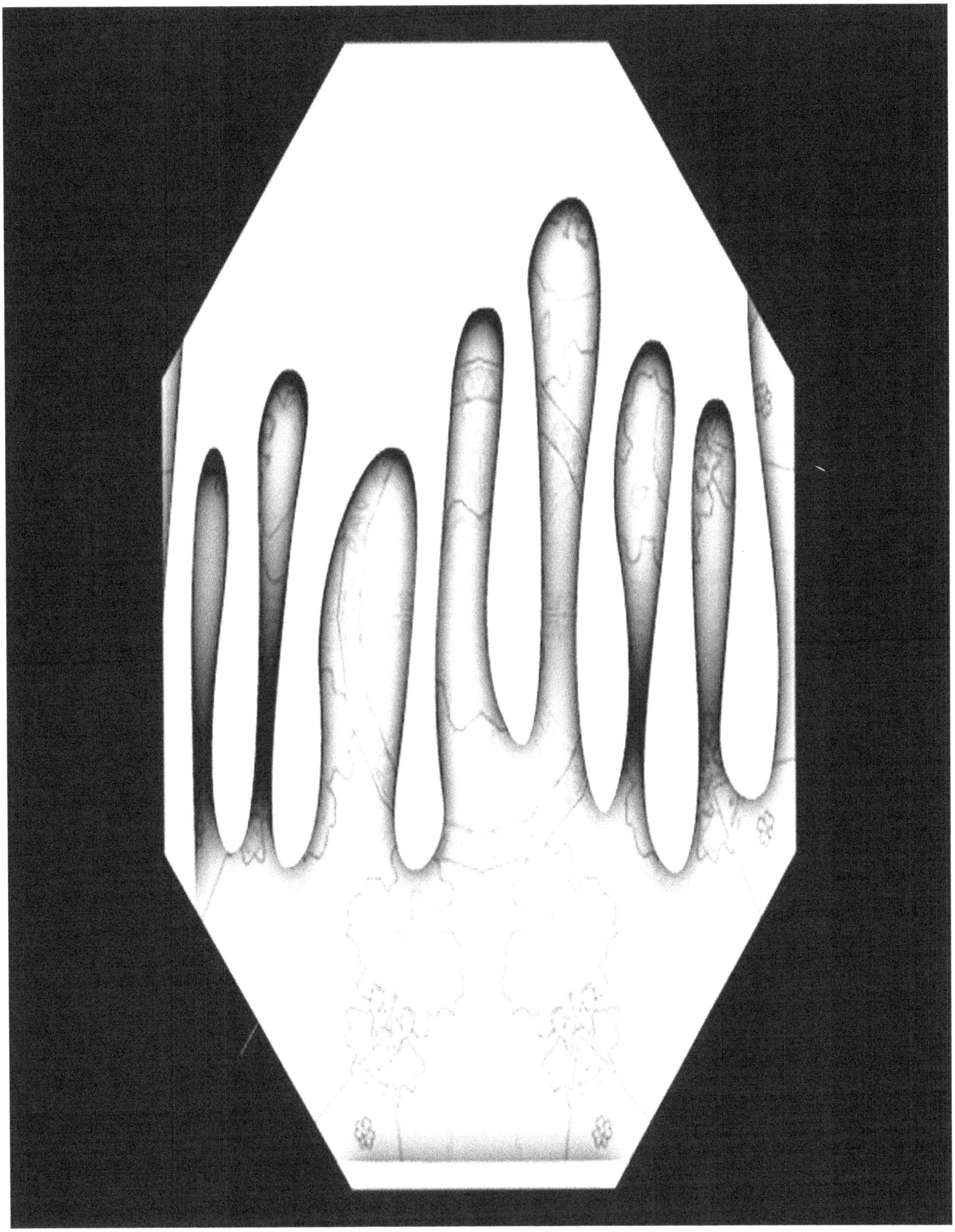

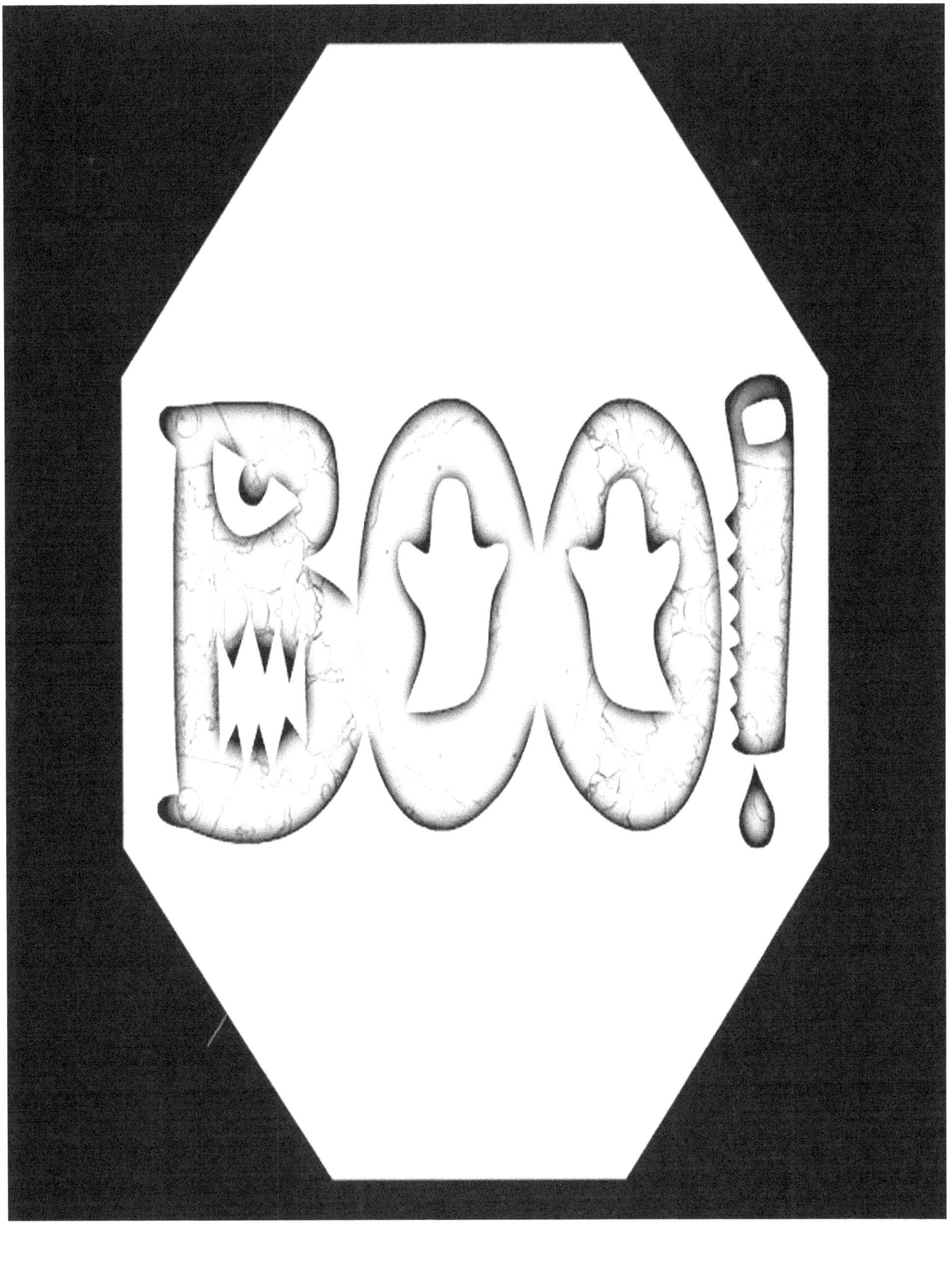
BOO!

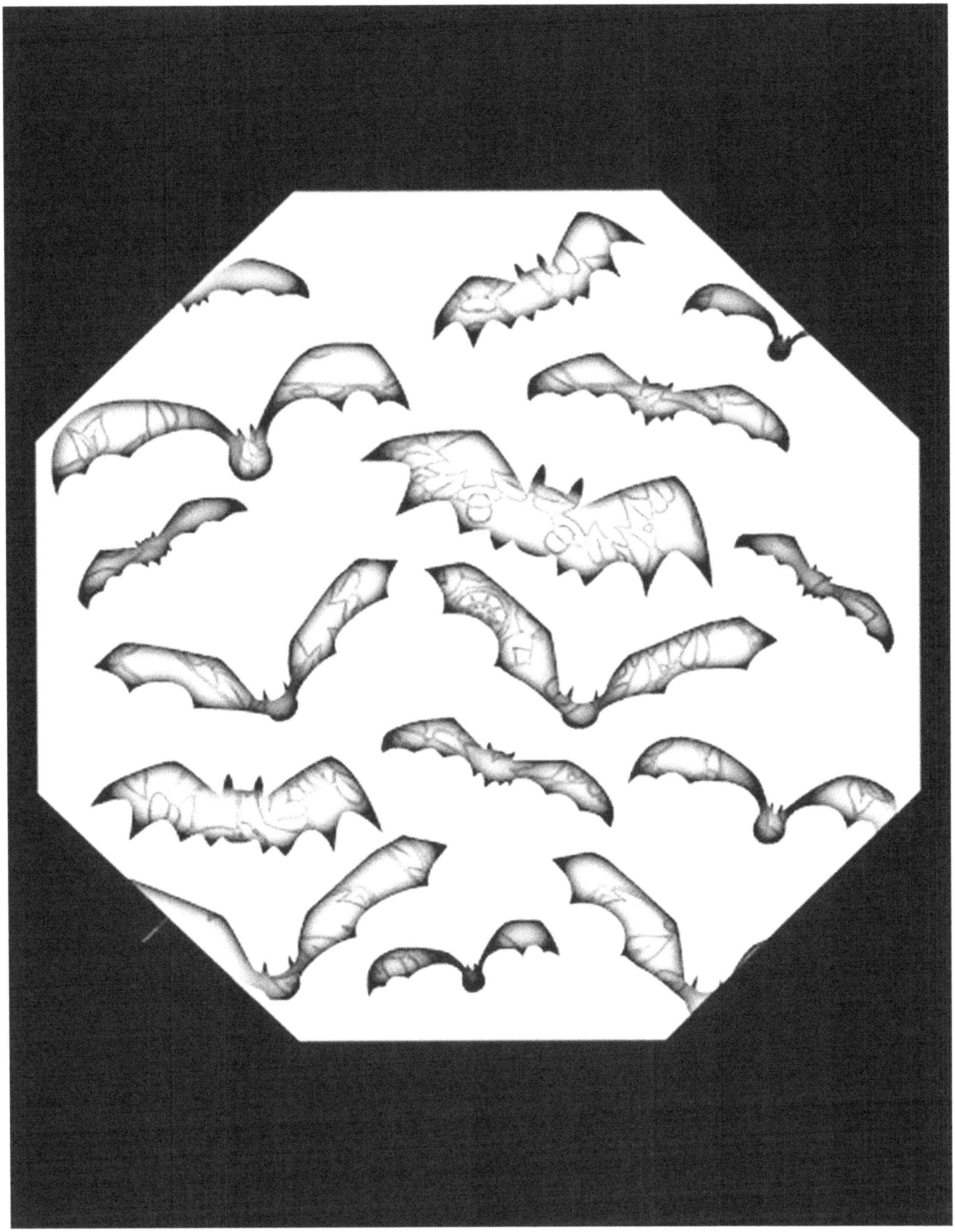

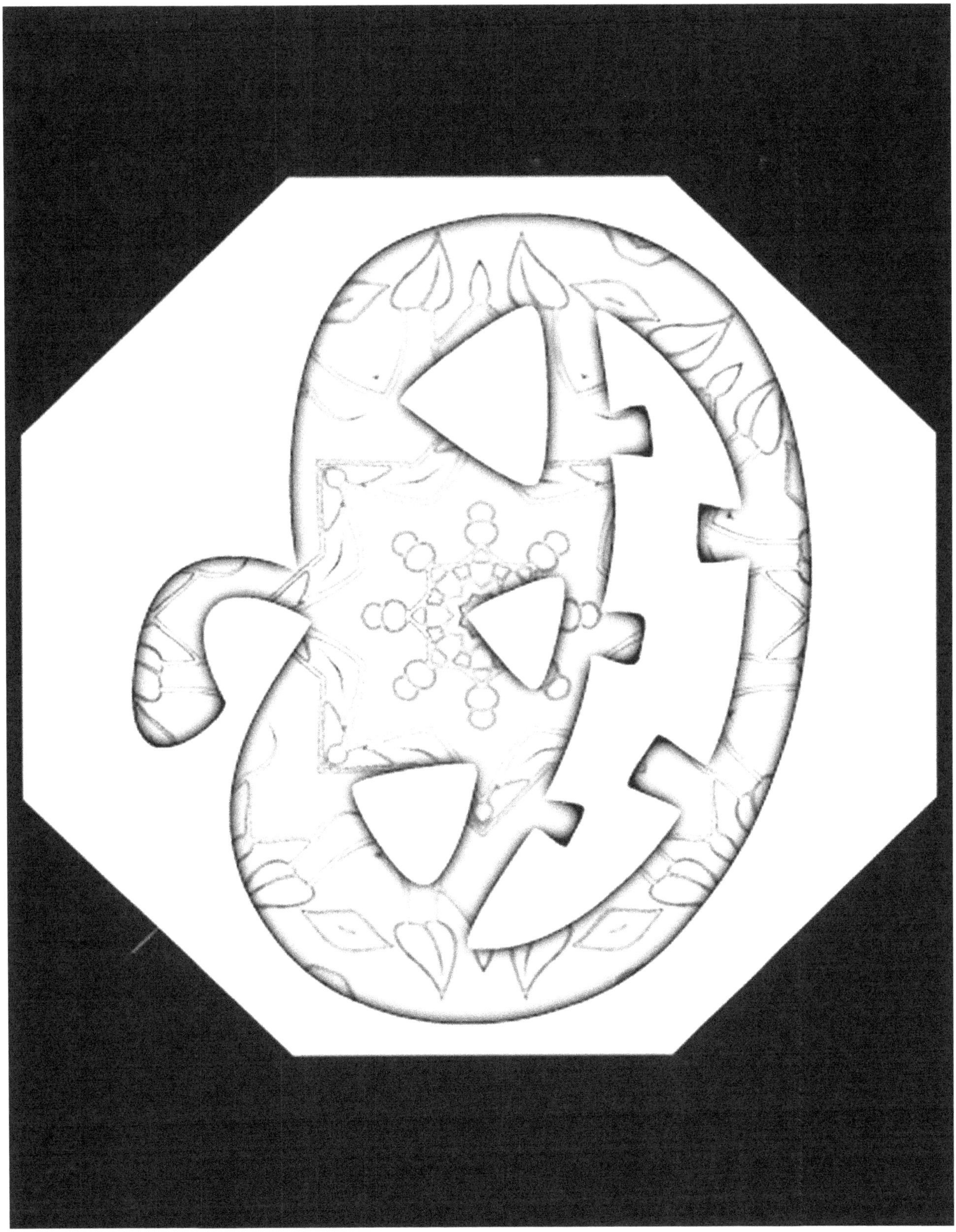

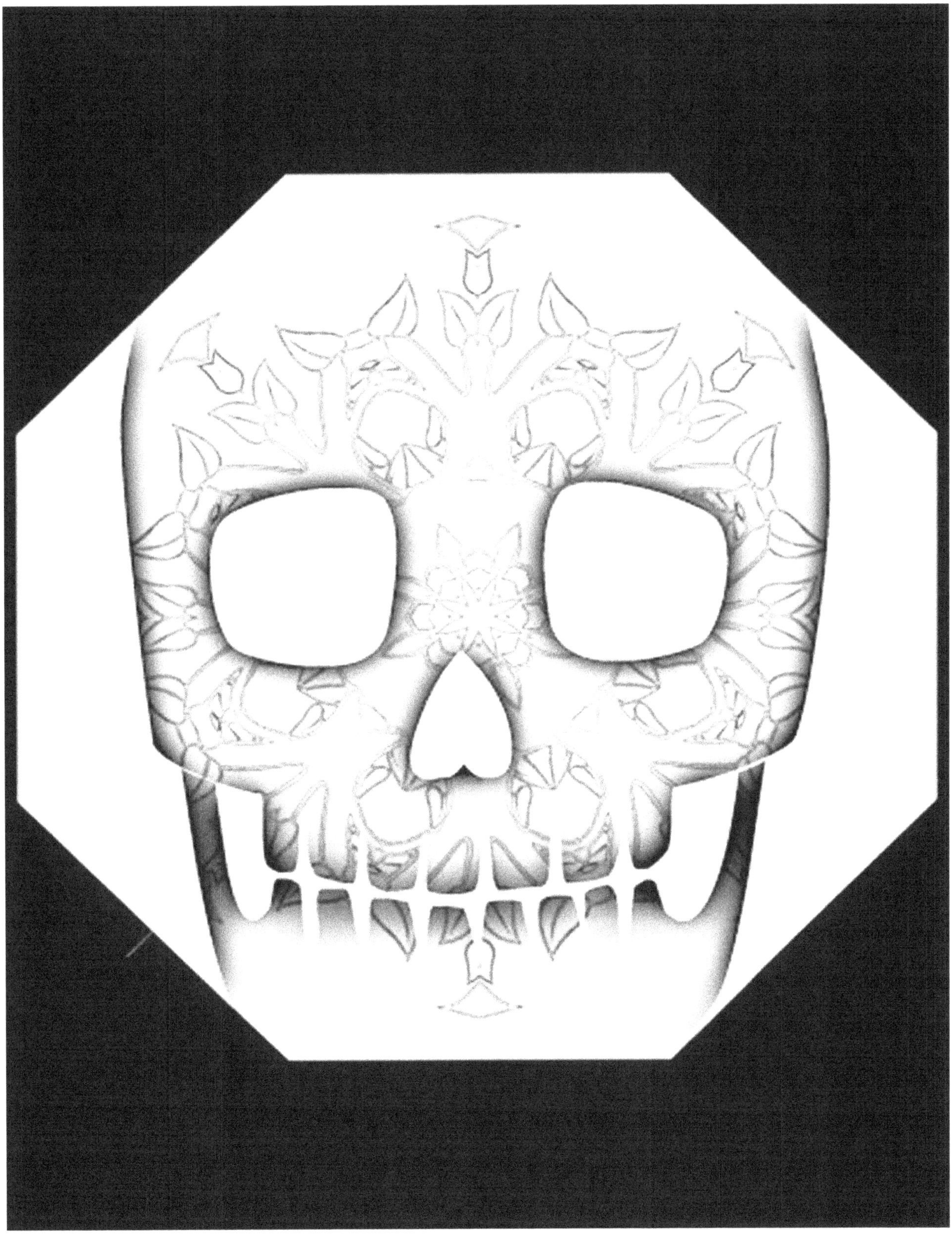

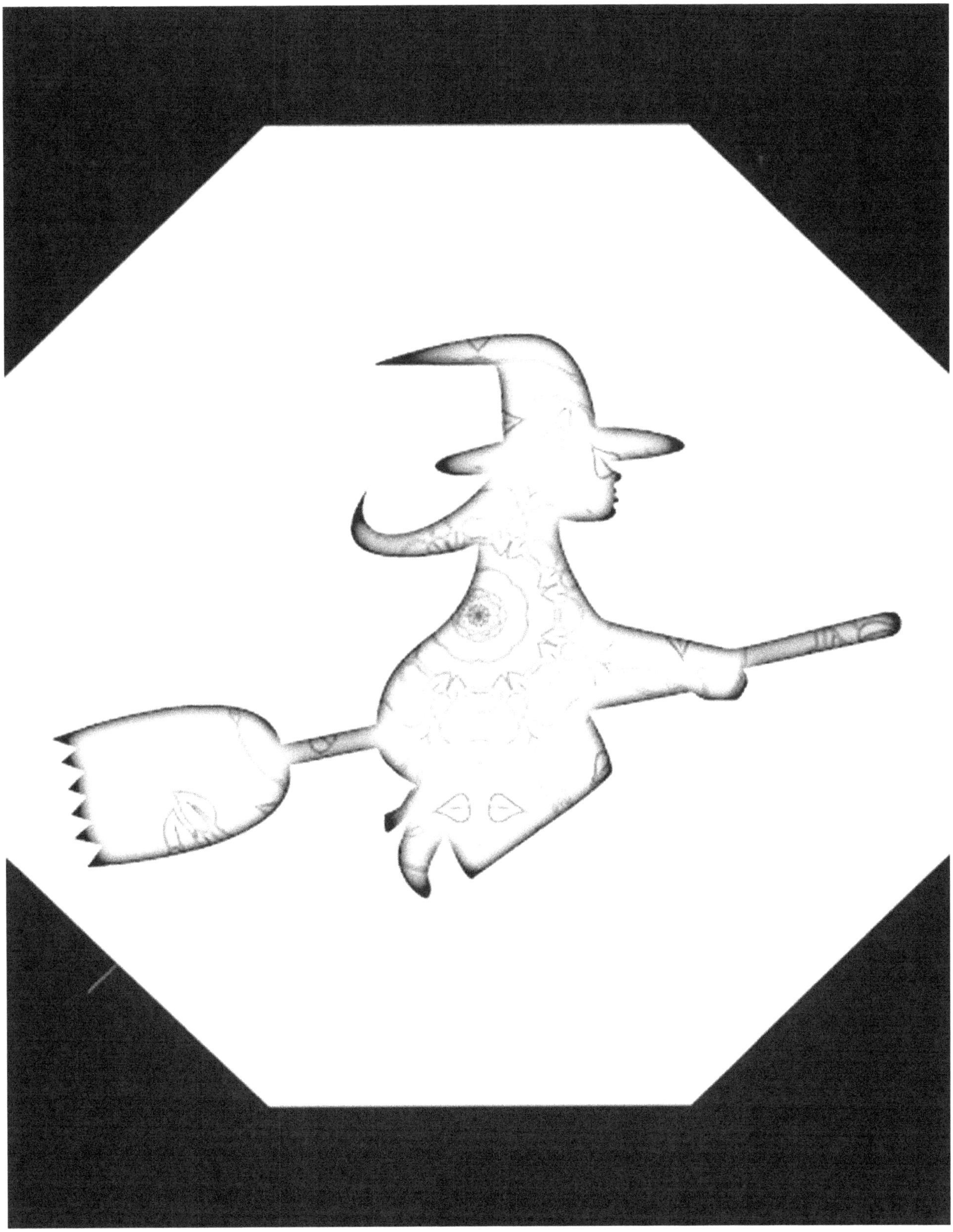

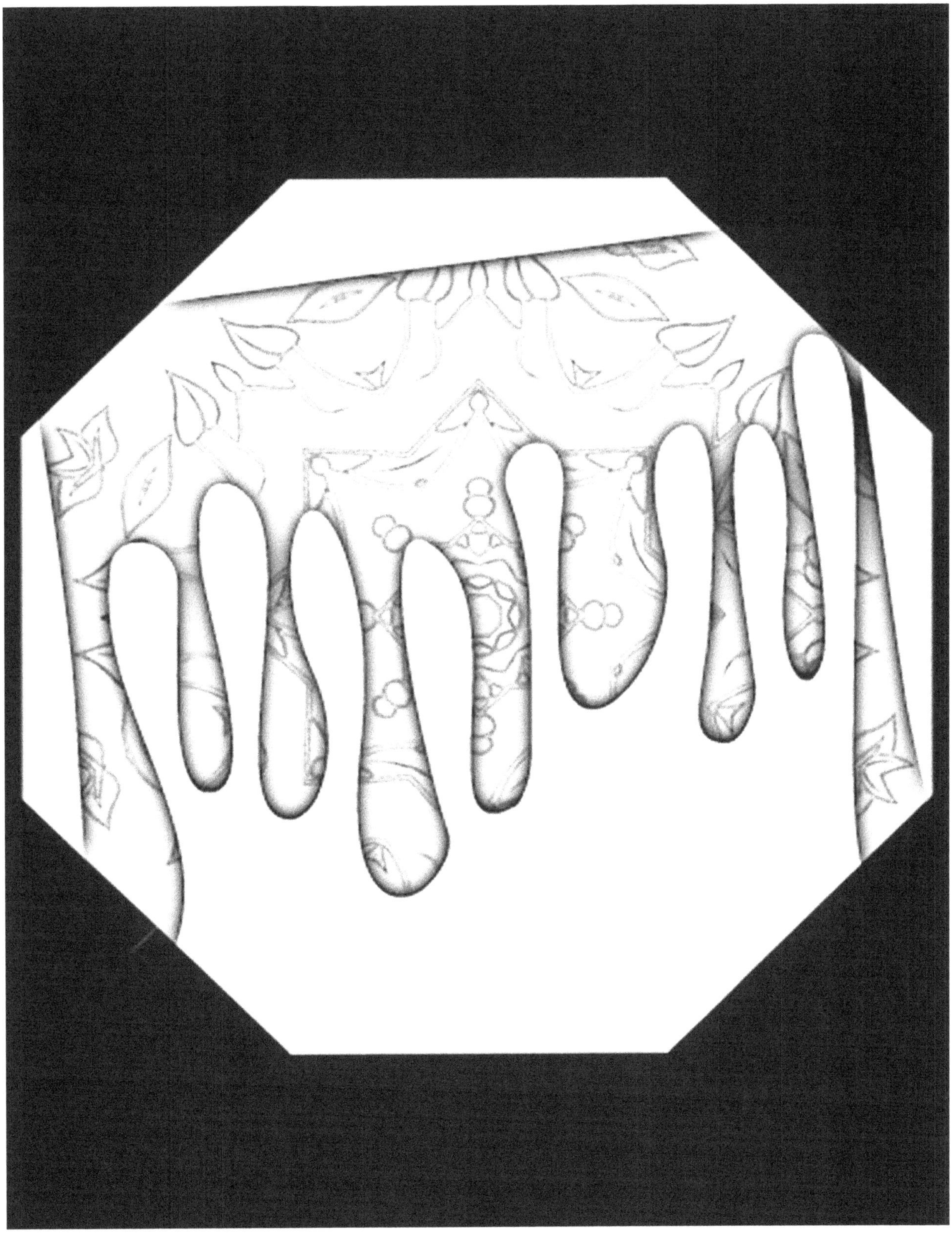

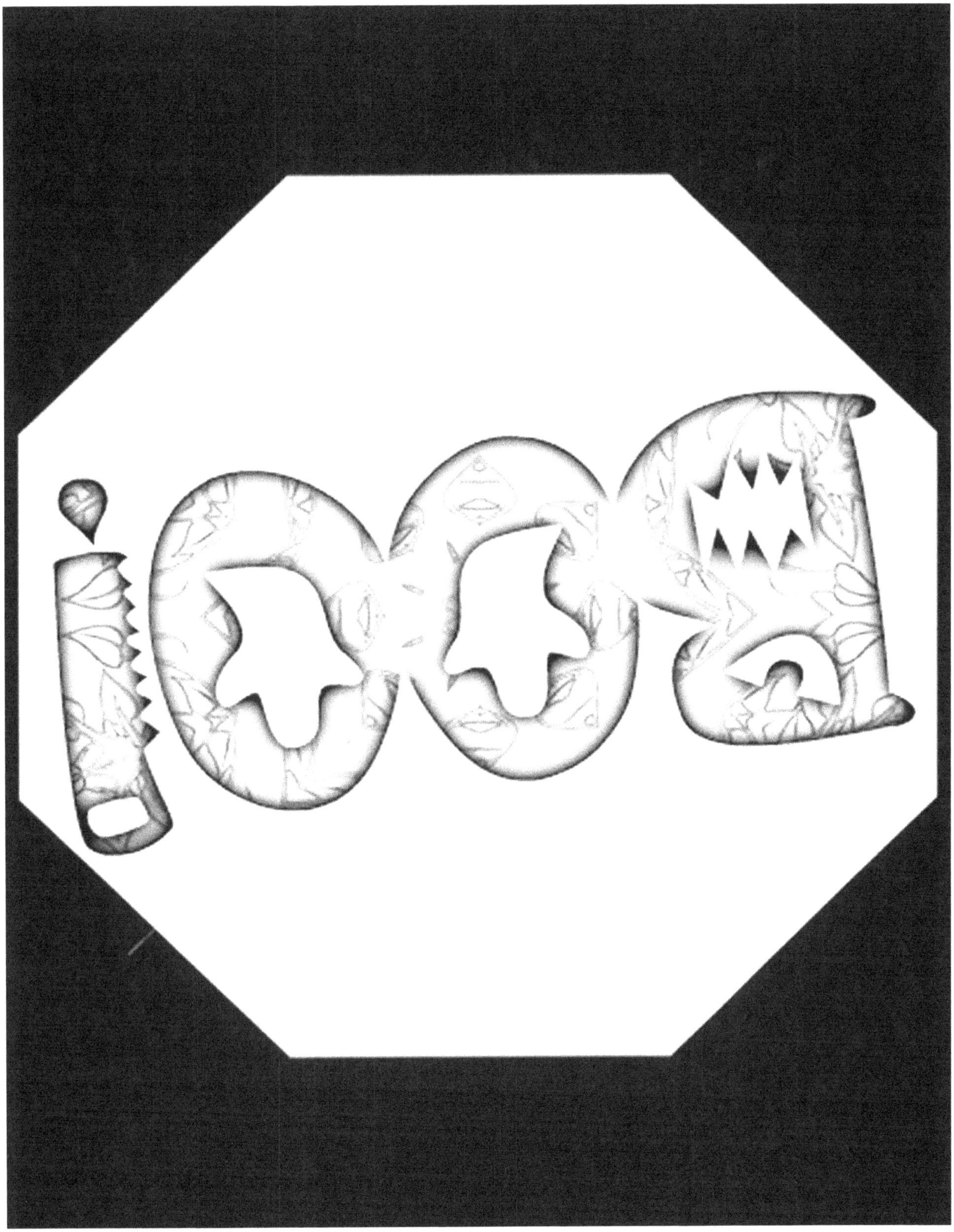
Boo!

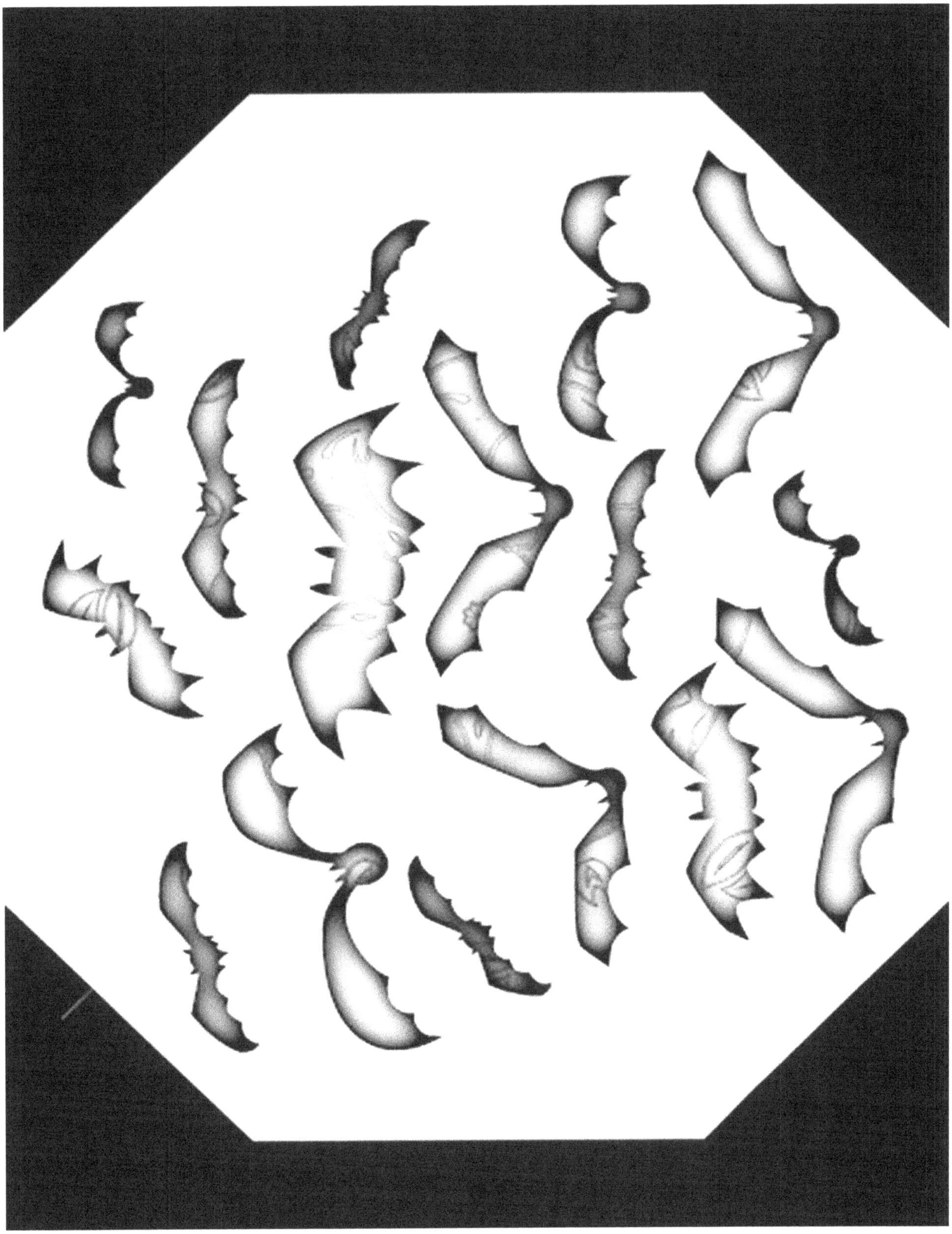

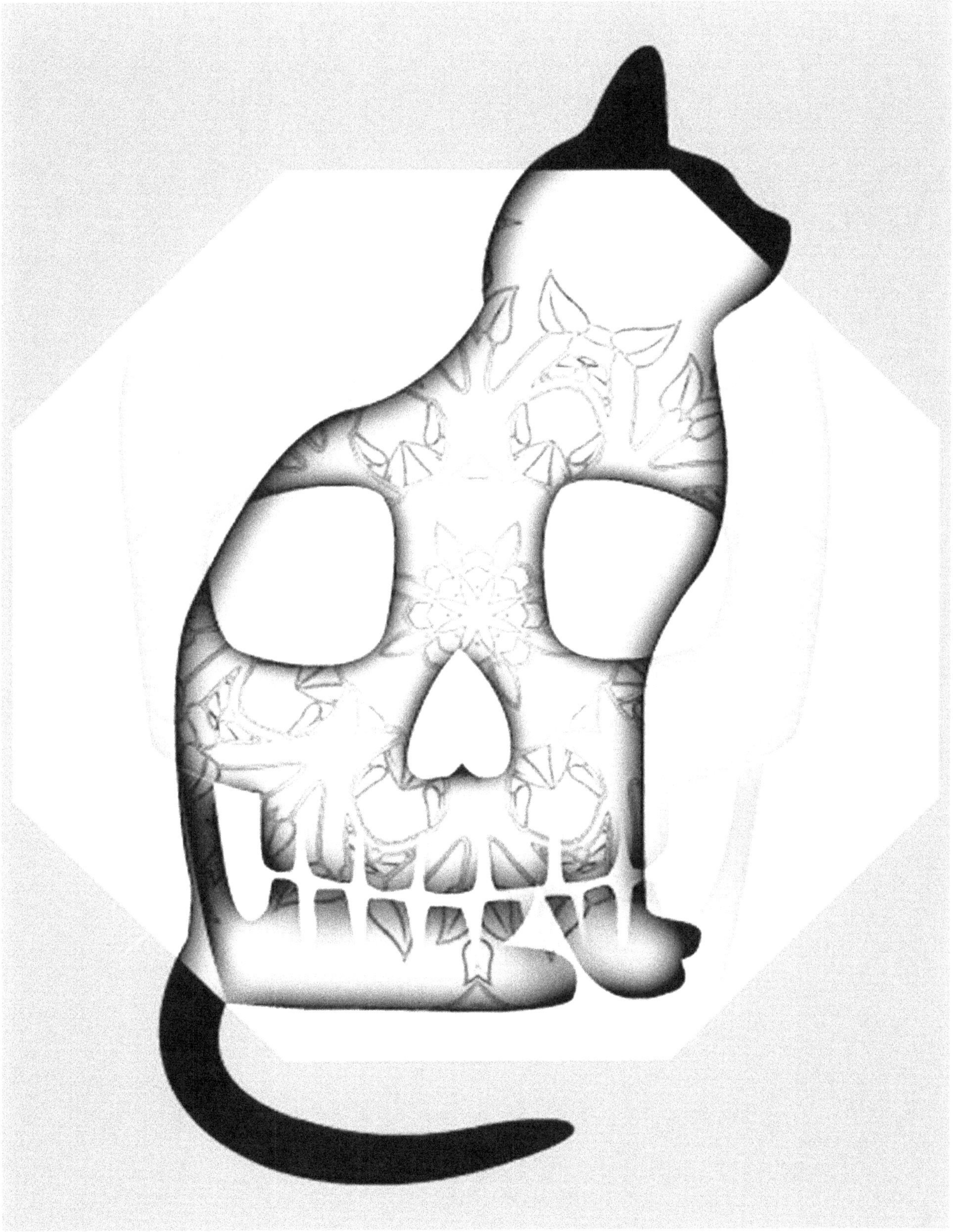

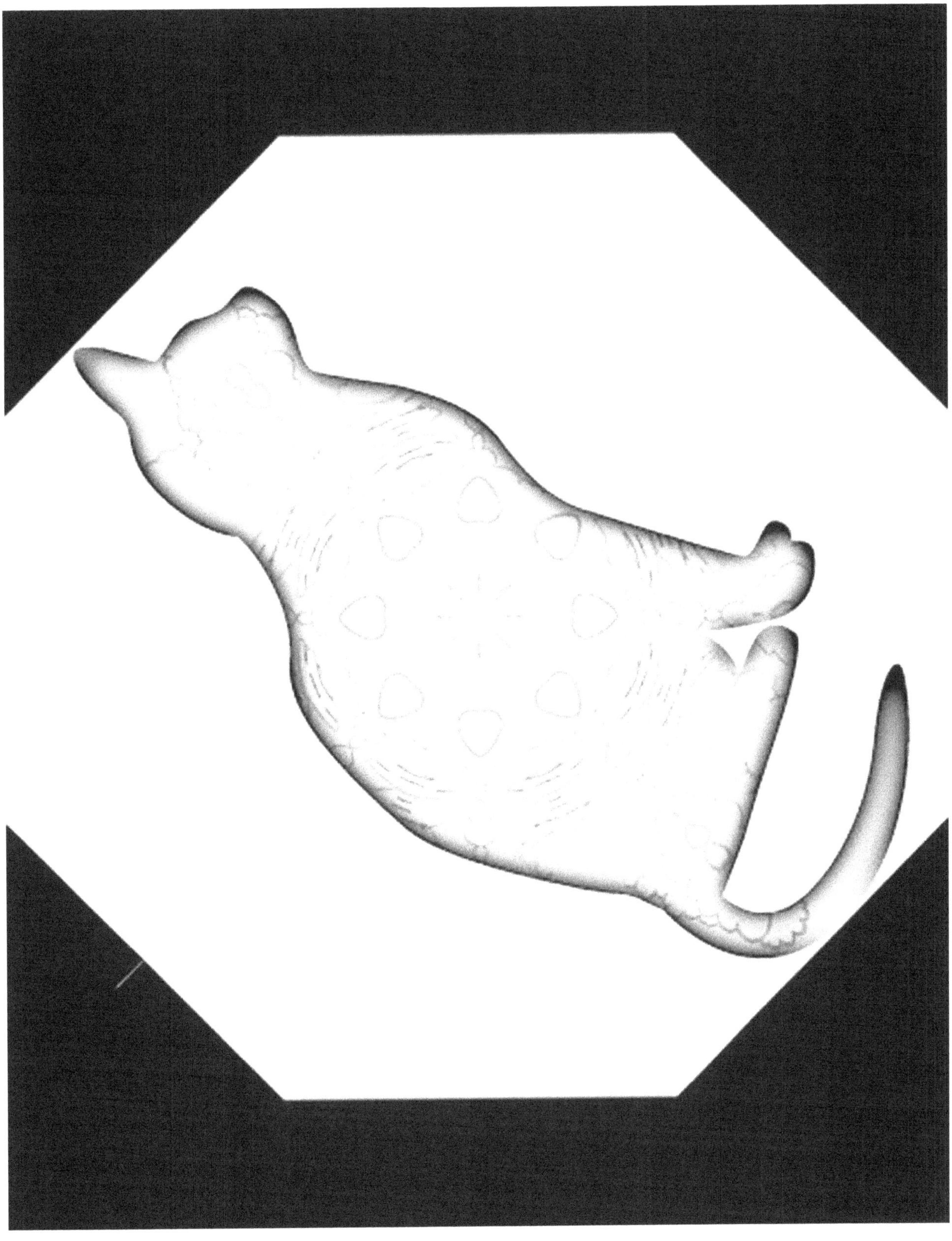

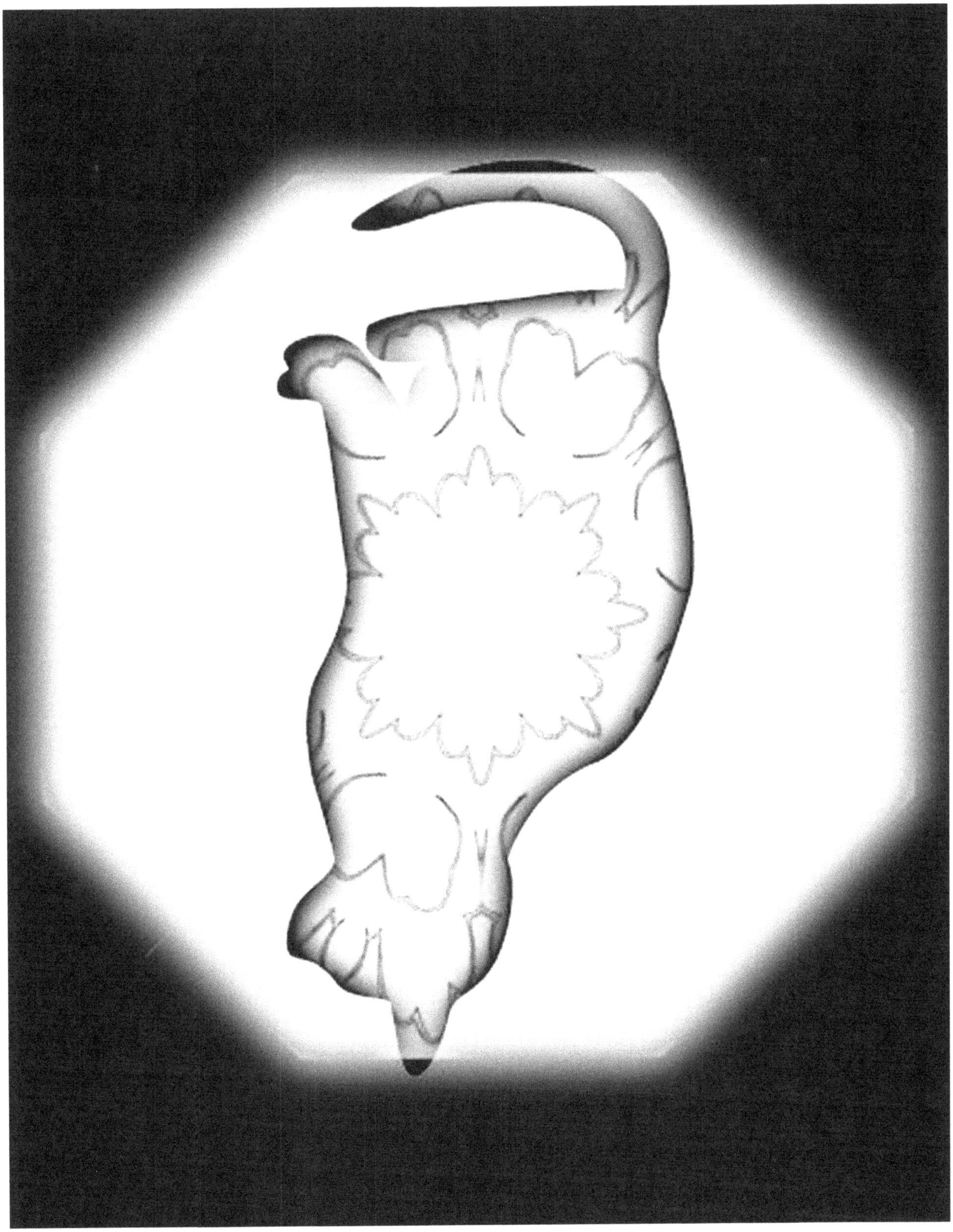

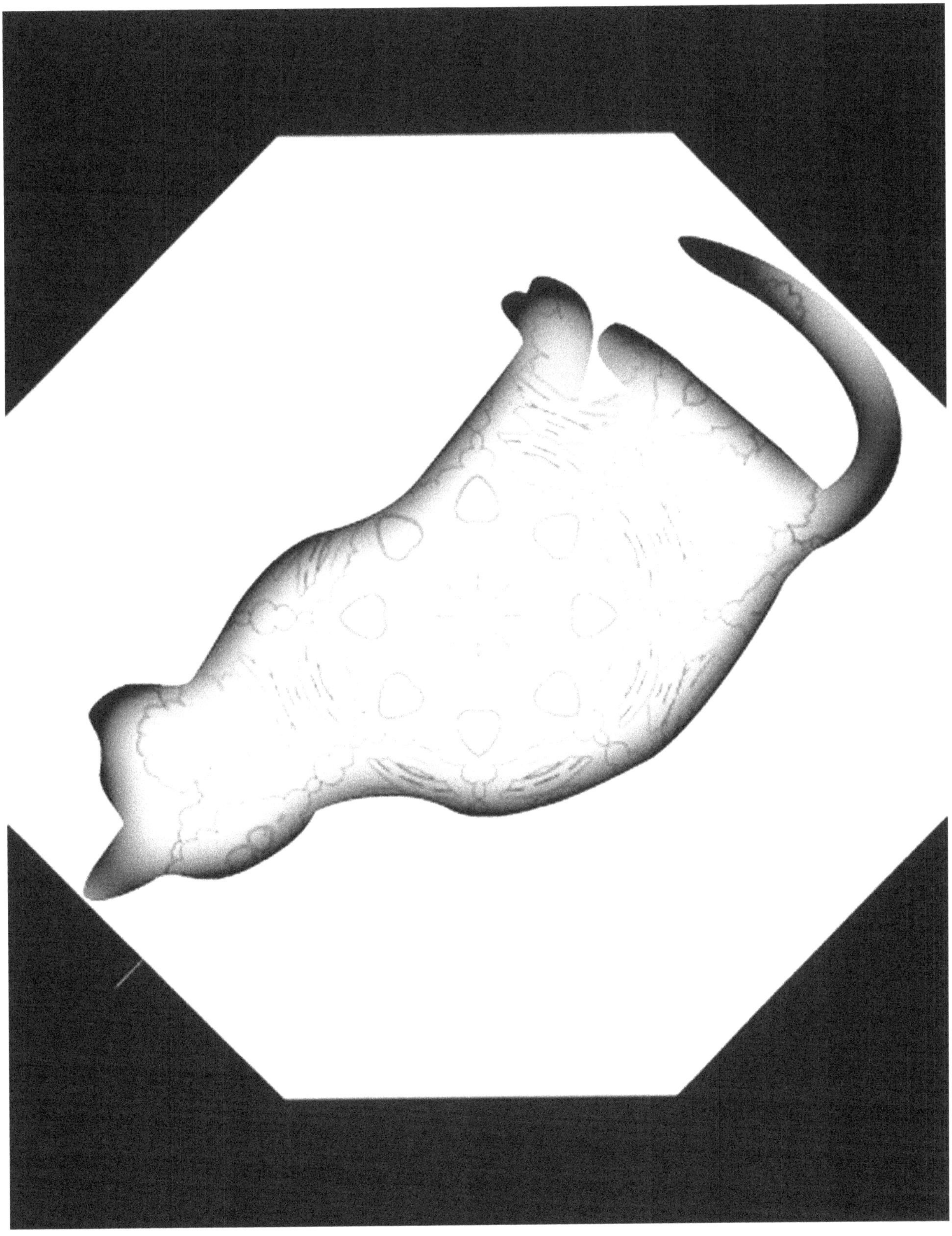

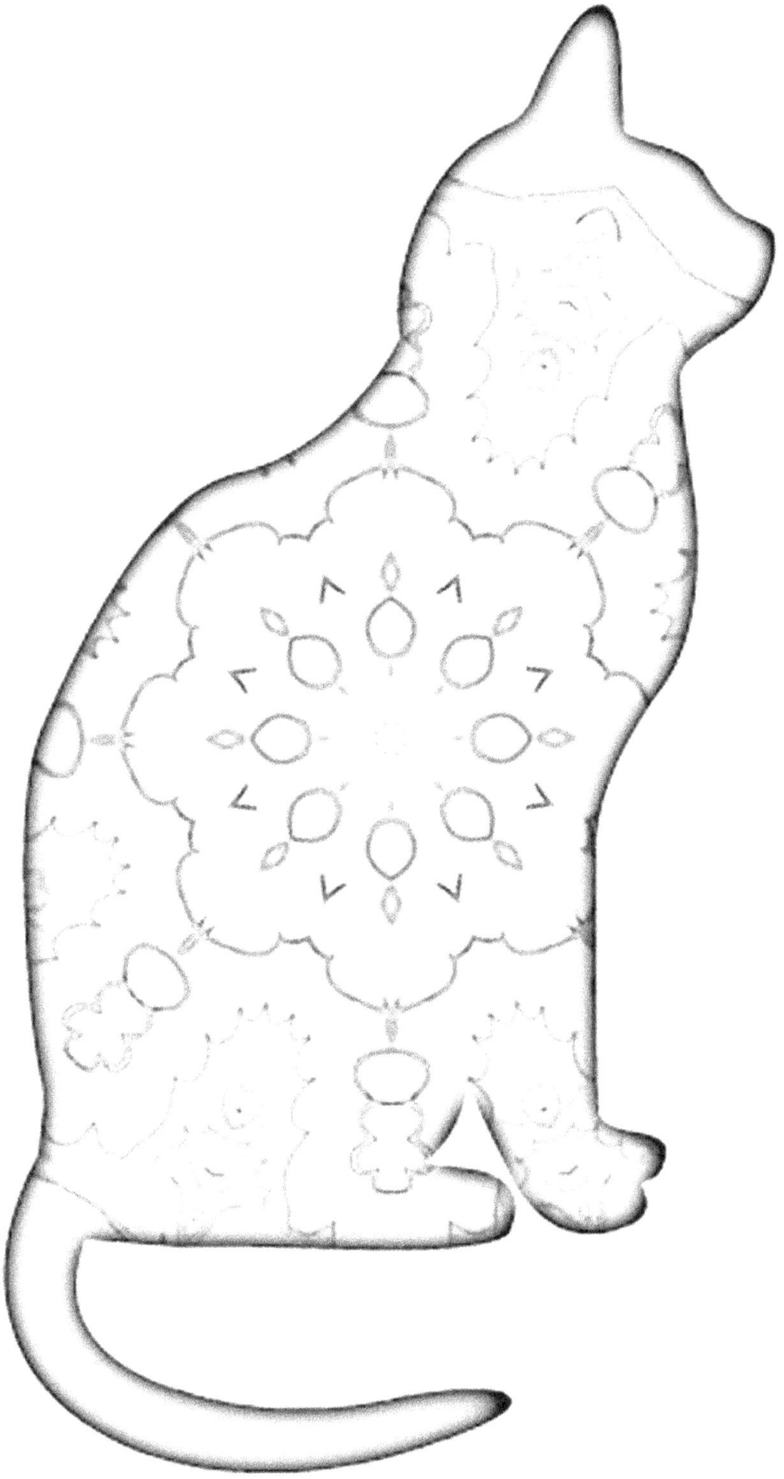

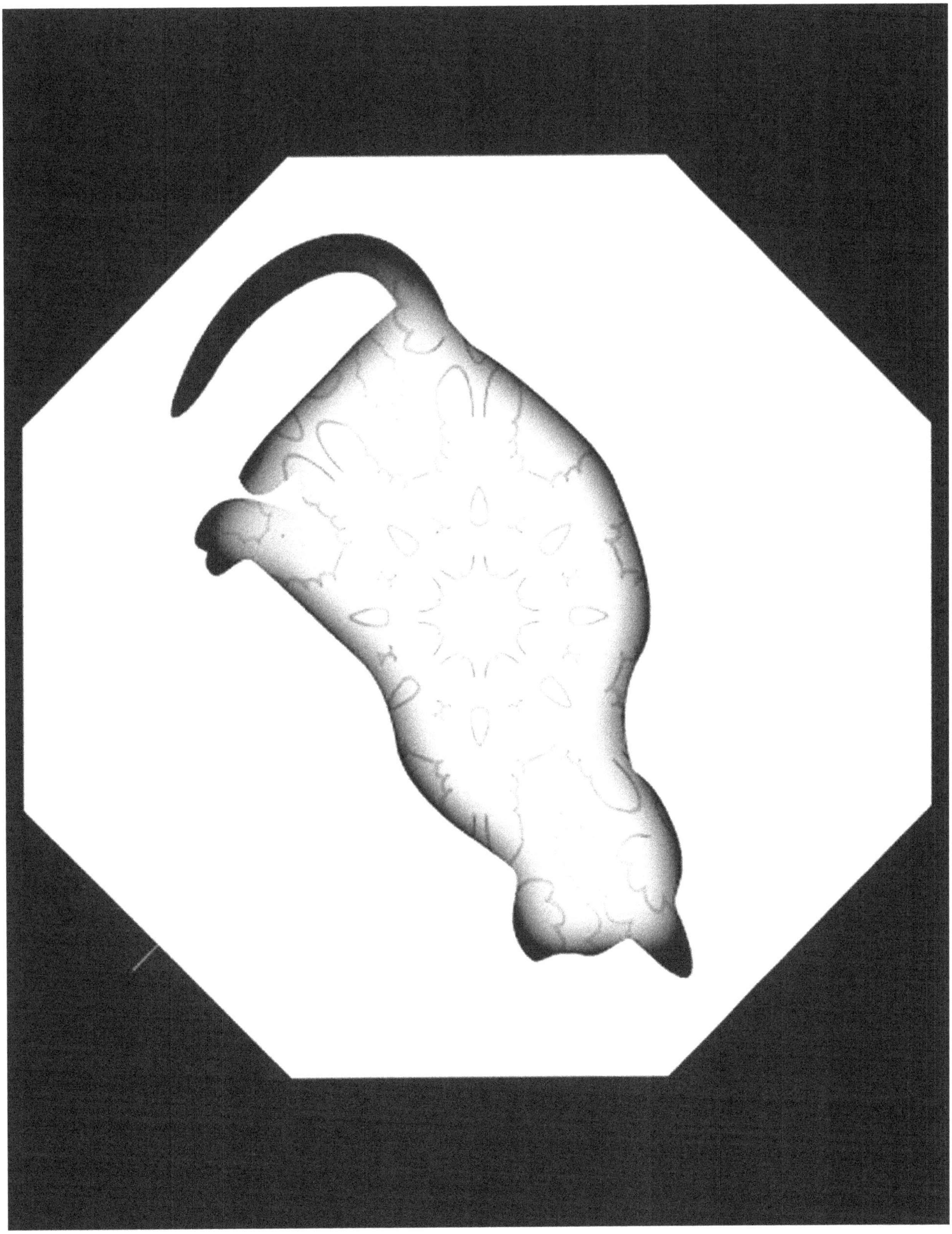

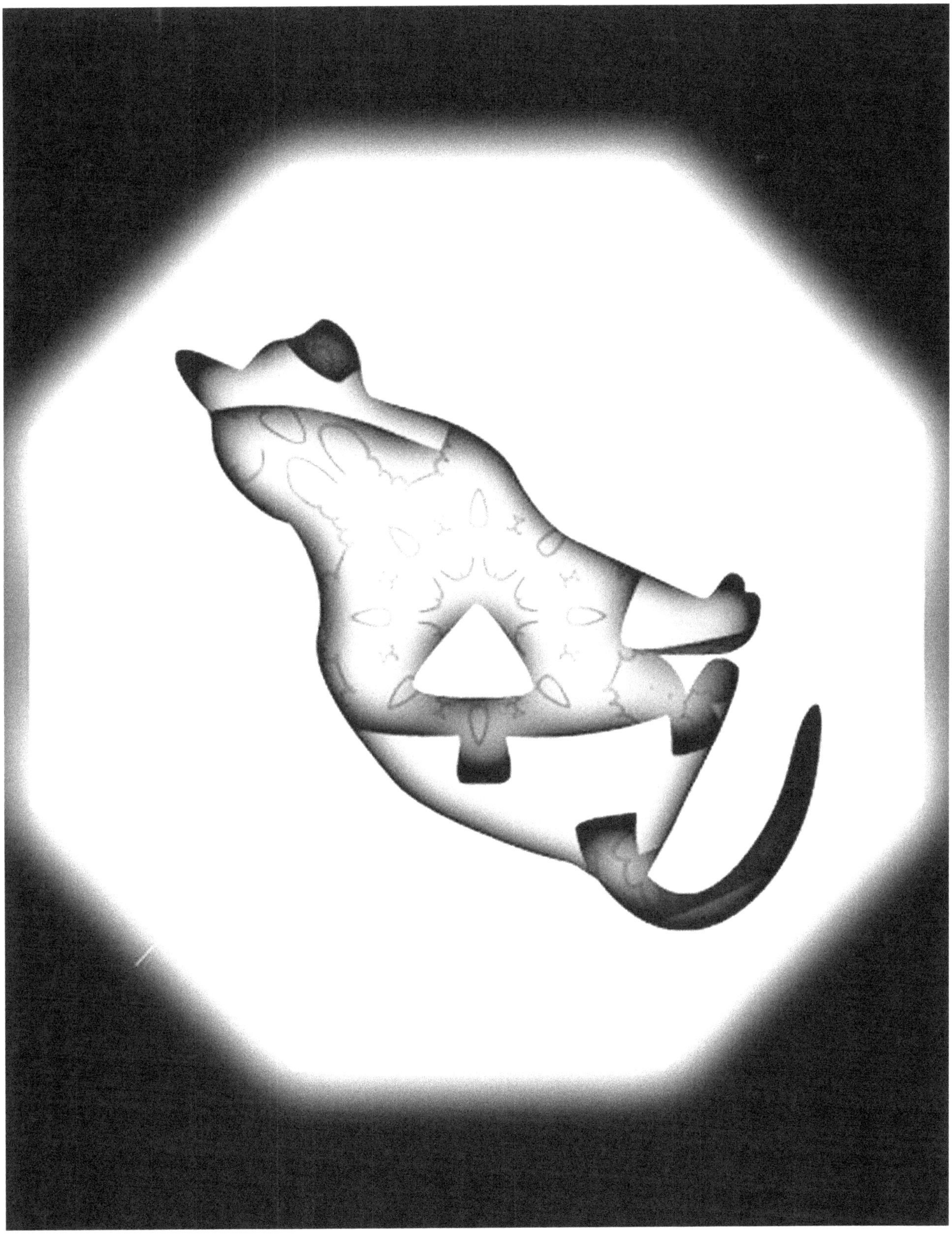

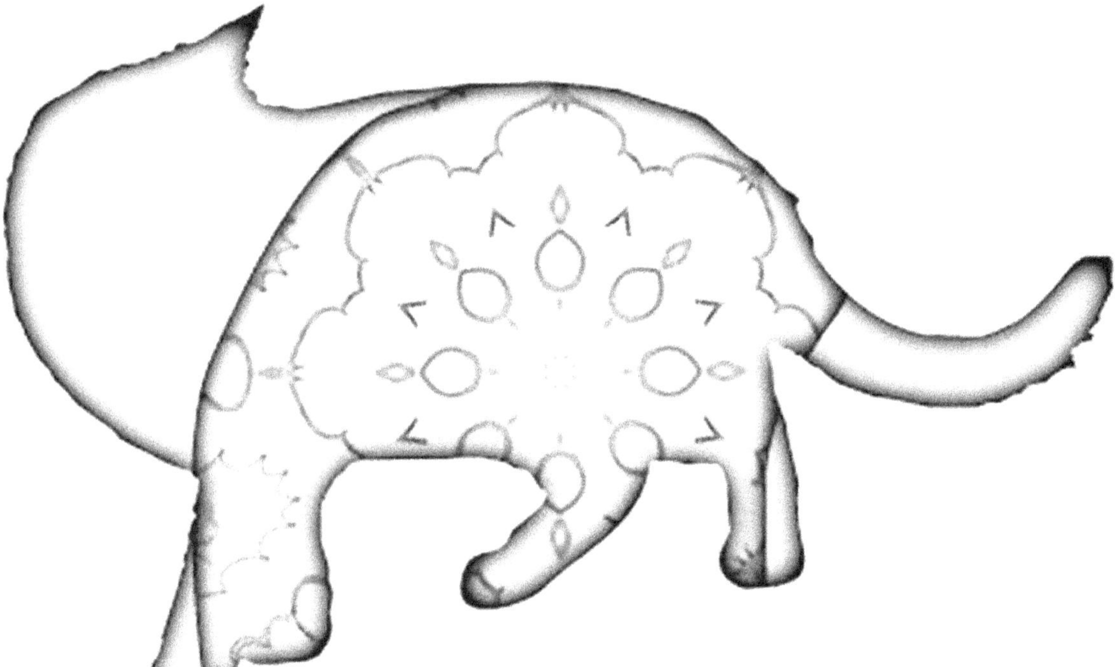

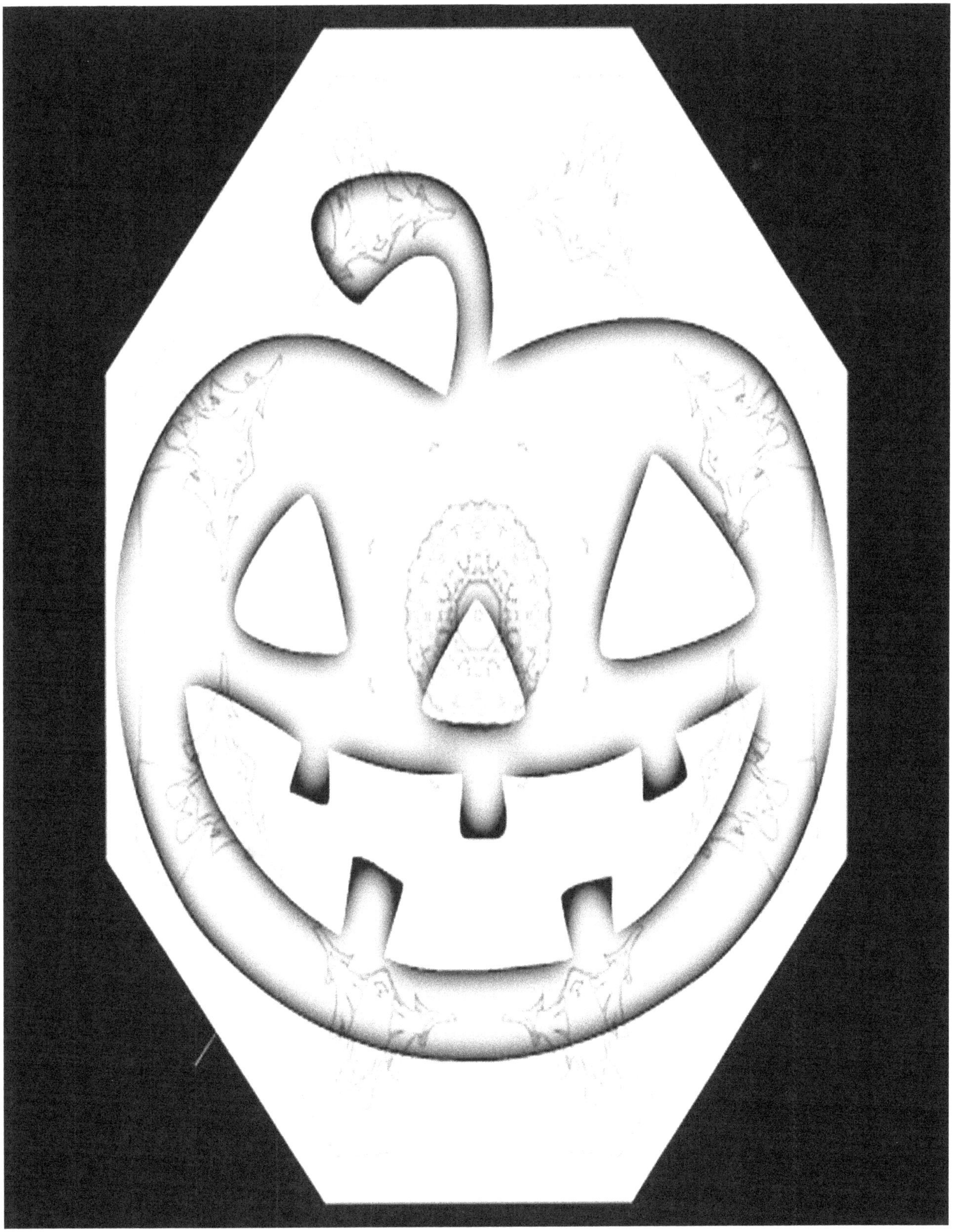

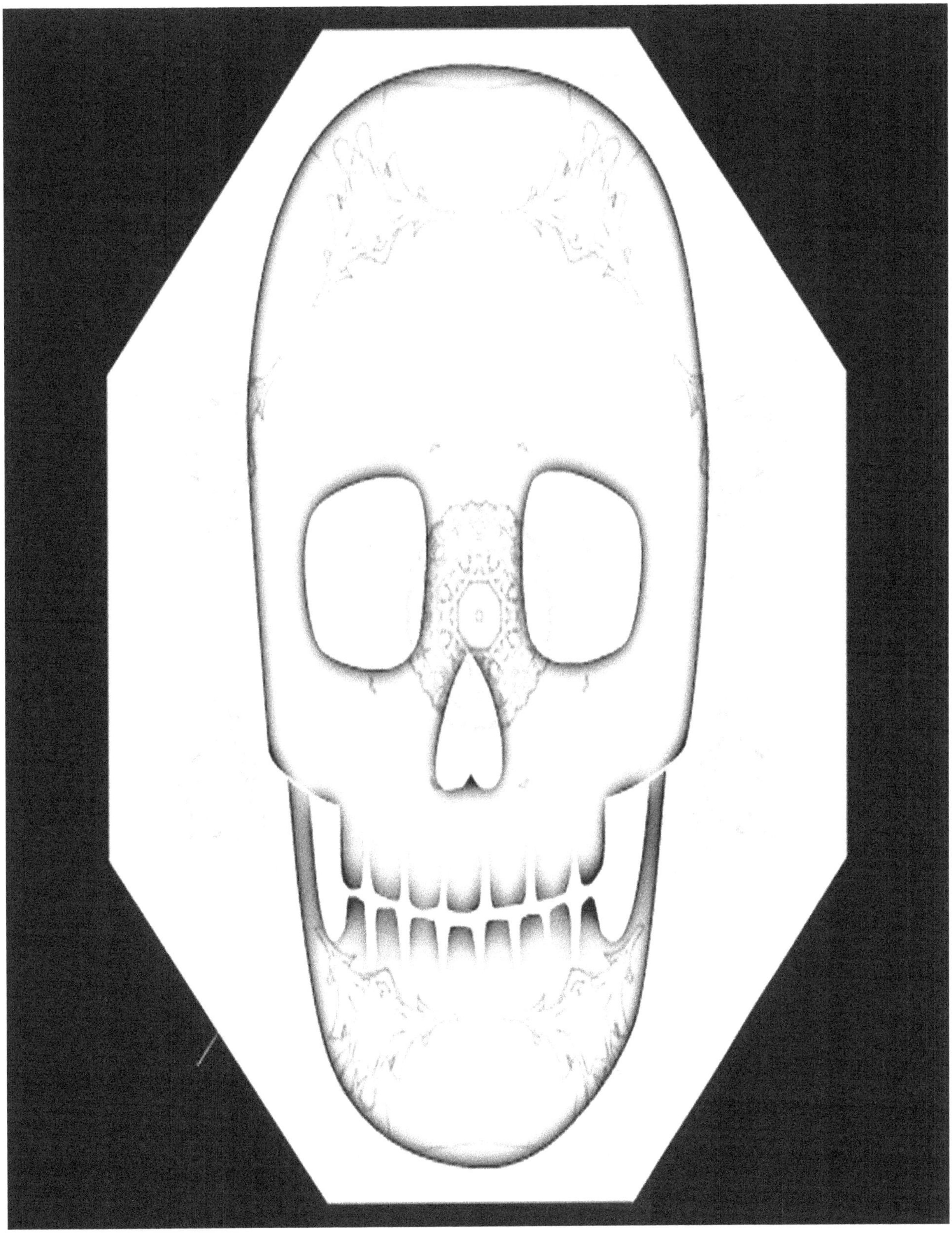

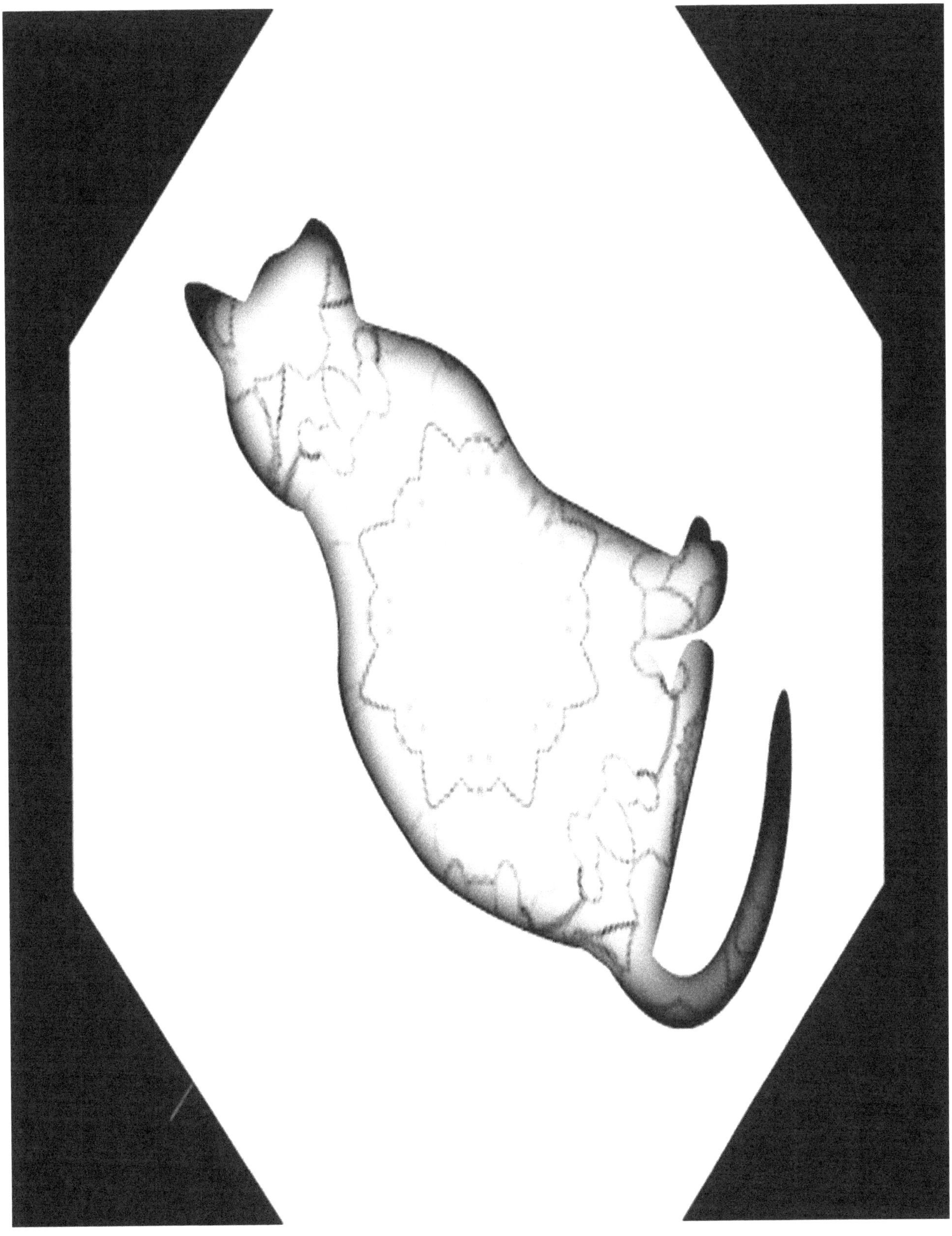

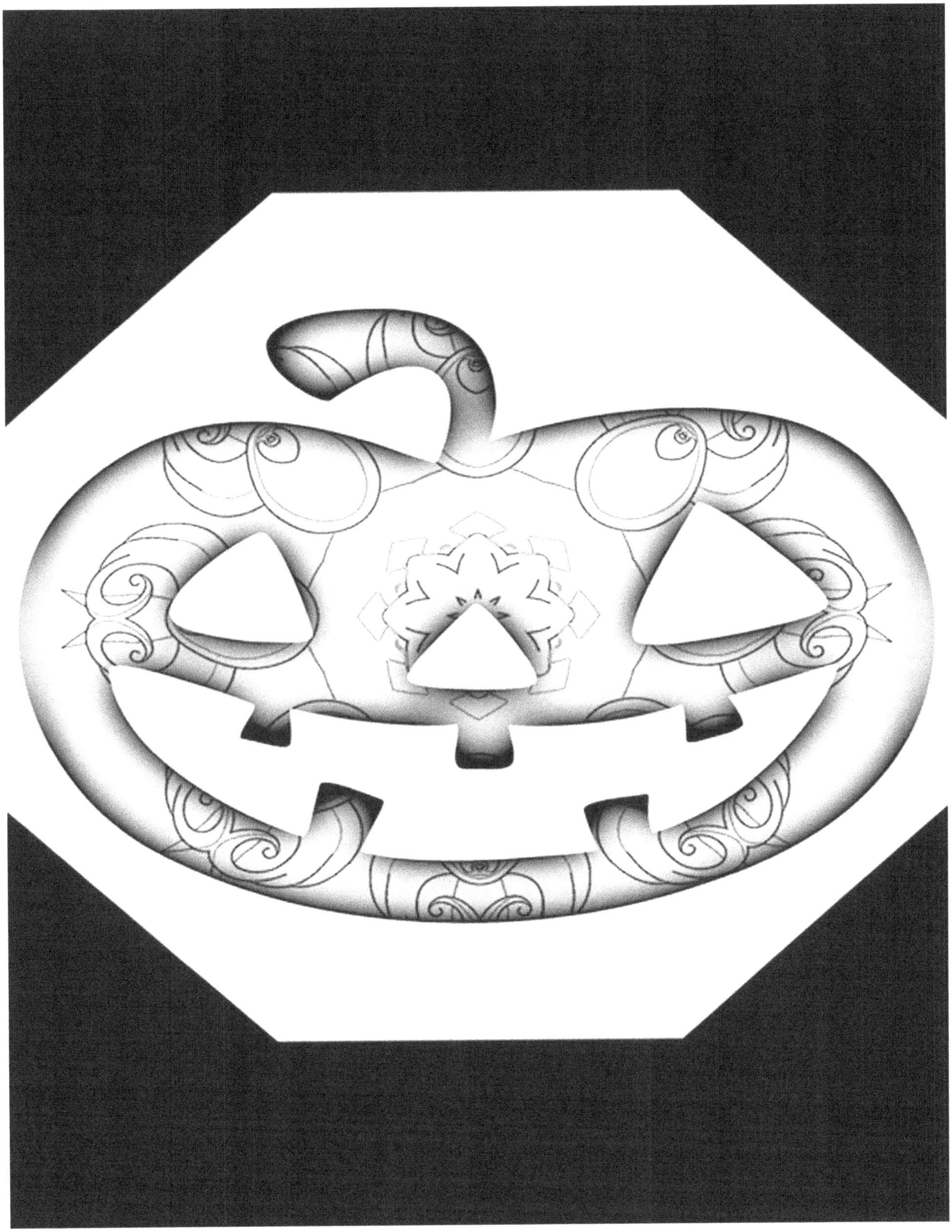

Note

www.ingramcontent.com/pod-product-compliance
Lightning Source LLC
Chambersburg PA
CBHW080651180526
45168CB00008B/3381
9781518674297